Occasionals

Also by Carol Watts:

When blue light falls 1 & 2 (Oystercatcher, 2008; 2010)
this is red (Torque Press, 2010)
Wrack (Reality Street, 2007)
brass, running (Equipage, 2006)
alpha*betise* (intercapillary editions, 2005)

Occasionals

Carol Watts

REALITY STREET

Published by
REALITY STREET
63 All Saints Street, Hastings, East Sussex TN34 3BN, UK
www.realitystreet.co.uk

First edition 2011
Copyright © Carol Watts, 2011. All rights reserved.
Cover image by the author: *January, WC2* (2011)
Typesetting & book design by Ken Edwards

Printed & bound in Great Britain by Lightning Source UK Ltd

A catalogue record for this book is available from the British Library

ISBN: 978-1-874400-52-3

Thanks to Caroline Bergvall, Robert Grenier and Rod Mengham for exchange and
conversation.

Versions of some poems have appeared in *Veer Away, Signals Magazine* 4, *Poetry Wales* and
Penumbra; and were recorded by the Poetry Center, San Francisco in March 2007. My
thanks to all involved.

To wish to remember that every year is a change if it is to be considered historically.
Every year is a change if it is to be considered historically.

Gertrude Stein, *Lucy Church Amiably*

1   autumncuts

|

So sit down with your green tea
as if this was your last day, leave
the ledgers unfinished and overdue,
and tell me what you take with you,
now, the sounds of instruments ringing
on pavements, a crow mulling over
trails of aeroplanes, everyone out
in the town, and sirens going.
Not enough to take that flickered.
Light and the lift of it. Spiders hang
in mating season, gorged bodies
weighted there, still, not washed out
by the rain, these last three days.
Hydrangeas shoot pale green flowers
at the end of the season as before it.
You could turn it on its head. Think
it does not end here. Steam blows
and unfurls, without the cold to catch it.
Your tongue will burn. In the kitchen
something rolls around, the engine
starts and creeps out across the block.
I see my hands are like hers, but older.
The fly zubs at the window. You will
be fined for lateness, need to clear
things. Stacking, the blue late
September, and filaments shining
between the glazing. Waiting for
replacement, by someone else, words.

23 SEPTEMBER 2006

II

No they do not arrive. Rain is falling,
in rushes, a thousand fingers. Pok pok
in the bucket, or is it butt, where someone
is collecting. Sun through the slat is enough
to confuse. It is *that* Sunday, perhaps.
It would be a relief to think it might not be,
a weight of future eyes. My eyes. His
have a small brown fleck, does it grow,
is it cause. To fret, neighbours move internally
a preparation which sounds like thunder,
in small accretions. But muted, as if furniture
is a comfort. Crowds applaud downstairs.
The scent of tomatoes in the week, just picked,
was I paying for that more than the taste,
remembering him standing there. Making
long straight lines with a drainpipe.
Now he would have been shaking the trees.
Get the apples down and wrap them for winter.
Newsprint. But he is still here, in Albi, his
cold comes over. Hot and the mouth
is a cathedral, sometimes scalded into vaults.
That will last for days, live to regret. Unthinking.
Birdsong in the rain, it makes a route out, or
good anticipation, eight-thirty, trust it, light
pulls up its skirt. Long, ankles, or heavy, more
provocative. The teacher with musk perfume
and makeup. Blue yellow. We sang every morning,
where the girl fell from the ropes. Tooth in tooth out,
shining parquet, up against the wall. *Hopefulness.*

24 SEPTEMBER

10

III

Fizz went the apples on a high branch. Too close
and fired up. The canned children below. Already
it is later, and ahead. Breath in a cold breeze,
wrapped against it, stamping feet, the smoothness
of skin, taut. Pores can be geometric. She tenses,
friendship swings on a high wire as high as it can.
Go asking. Buying rings with imaginary karma,
many years before, a moonstone tending to peach,
as if it had spent time ripening, I forget. The meaning,
like flesh, exchanged. Small seeds glow, tremble
on the wires, cars growling with contentment,
the season comes to itself, where sleep is a true
possibility. And not the dark. Will you just move
it on, he asks, and sends water. Pouring, folding
over itself, the house groans, creaks. Perhaps
the sun cools to help us out. Roofs and leaves
absorb, make nothing of it, mosses on one side,
but not the other, the wavier. He packs up to make
music by the railway, a path of sleepers, built. Ivy
may reach her perfect garden, no no, he shouts,
it will make my eyes. Water. They steamed
where they hung, yellow globes, bursting. Bark
singed, too close. Tendrils out. Red, mauve, curling,
daring to touch her brick. Mine is a waterfall,
green and powdery, broken stems, difficult.
To tell where it starts, introducing a few words in
Yoruba, the boy who spoke. Writ of prohibition.
Does not find them. Alongside write: engrave, carve.

25 SEPTEMBER

aking in the night keeps everyone restless.
d it always, instances of confession, dreaming
of lines and inches, fitting, and then unbearable.
Pitch. Perhaps tinnitus is protection from this
fundamental ringing. La la la can't hear you, he
said yesterday. Listening takes something from
bodies, it is a propelling. When is the brain ready
for patience. Running along, as if it could be
rain, then a door. Closing, deft in the quiet, mist
fades in the afternoon, not yet burnt off. Taste,
when new to the city, yeast and sweet potatoes,
was it sulphur or a derivative, they lived by gasworks,
the Becks of Becktown. Lightning strikes and switches
the hemispheres, left does the operation of right.
It leaves metal burns, could be filigree, rivets, or
eternity. Rings, as evidence. That lawyer predicted
only a bolt would end him, and it did, not before a
fight. Trees and buildings send up fingers,
affinity, hoping to draw it down. Bodies do too.
Siphoning. It said thunder but is altogether too gentle.
More difficult to draw down calm, whittle silence
from the greyness, puffed with sky traffic and
cleaning. Even empty is lenticular, making speech
from another angle. Forces are grainier with age,
like you could cut them. Tolling twelve, bells in
another warp, almost reluctant, and the steadiness
of iron. Tongues, like a b or d, beginning, and then
cavernous, you could sleep safe there, she didn't say.

25 SEPTEMBER

V

Seeing all the children trying. Braided hair, with
a long line of copper. Coils. Of black. Keep to the
right. Tumbling and tressed up, gorgeous. Language
holds her in, she is guiding our way in the dark,
better than we could. Assuming our blindness, poverty,
ah. Line up please. We are learning persuasion, how to.
Write complicated sentences, where words rhyme
in product kitemarks. On the street, invasions of
advertising, with answering gunfire. LaLaLangue.doc,
cloistered corridors. Cool interior of that painted. Tree
of life, the distribution of birds, branching, it could.
Be wild, enormous. Look at the roots. Skin is
always social, even when intimate. Tattoo, a tree on
dusty walls. Secure, the word, making his mouth.
Discute. Try seclusion, even better. Sound
of water in the way it turns. In art we are tested
by the extent of shadow, shading is. Proficiency,
he imagines an extra r in worry, like a furrowed
face. It is his because he hears it. Why you are lucky
to be here. Veins breaking through, different from skin
is being broken, does it come. With age, a. Discrimination,
of kinds. Furocious machine, the wind, he wrote. Very,
very strong, like a birthright, were you scared. No,
I stood on the doorstep to taste it, the heat. Cars
move very fast. Sucking something from the children,
as if play offends. Is it important to assemble, store
remnants, without recognition. The dryness of grass in
late summer. The scent of crimson. Lip. Stick, sap.

30 SEPTEMBER

13

VI

There are constancies in parting, no two. The same.
Sun breaks through the window, skin expands in relief.
Still here, I can see. You, leaning in the black suit, sepia.
Warmth, a potential of black and white. Against
the drying nets, stench of salt. Photosensitive you are.
Laughter fans a tail in the garden. Blanching beans always
seemed serious labour, pulling the strings. Along the edge,
and into the water, for limited minutes. Forking sprays,
purple miscalculating sugar. Secret stashes, stores
of anything coming into. Ripeness, earth still. Attached,
red berries overwintering. Pomegranates, he says, are
hearts. Spurting, down to the hatch across. The way
through goosegrass, taking peas and carrots home.
Small girl, wrapped by the pound, butter in pats, slapped.
Rats got the bread, he said, it turned out to be your mother.
Burrowing in patisserie, we licked the cream. Horns, destined
for others, by the coal merchants. The cobbler's rheumy
dog. Shaped in sheaves, skull and crossbones footstone.
In the churchyard, imprinted, where the man with the bush
showed himself, she said. Rain arrives, in skeins, it would take
the breath from you, if you ran. With mouths open, the pain
in the chest. Flying, pears scattering, I know you, she shouted.
Flying, and gently coming down. Alight, in dreams without
oceans, always. A sign of turbulence. Did you see, we asked.
It was a large bush. Whitethorn, you can't bring it
in to the house. Spring Gardens was once a cholera pit.
In records, home. Neighbours moved to Australia, they were
dutiful to their mother. Knew my secret. Ungratefulness.

30 SEPTEMBER

VII

Cosas que pasan. Things happen. In the occasional,
without recognition. Risks run, tessellate. He would
burn her back, he says, his. Mother, into presence.
As if she would return to herself in his desire.
Too close. To see she might want in her own terms.
Horror is best domesticated, and we weep
vainly. When the wind swells, the plane enters sound
differently. Spins, the way a compass needle does,
finding. Direction, a lag catching, before it steadies.
What happens in an indrawn. Breath, on that scale.
A thunder clap, restarting. *If Living Is Without You*,
across hedge groins, privet privates. At night, chorus,
I Can't. We climbed the pines, he buried. Cut-out
pictures, leaving holes. The small incline was
freedom. Resin, bark, bending under weight.
It might pitch us. To the ground, coyotes falling
from the cliff. Followed by a rock, suspended.
Any More, plangent warbling. The hum of wings,
happens. Colour of a green beetle, catching. Light
between branches, this summer. Taped birdsong,
ticks in the sink bowl, shaken. Water trapped
in its own form, mild. Planetary skin, float, tasting.
Clear borealis, we went to look, treading it. The cliffs
rose, let my limbs get me there and back. About
to dive and you shouted, what about. The book,
panic. Caves, where children swing. In times of
famine. They stockpile. Supplies, mouldering
in deserted buildings, infrequently visited. Yes.

2 OCTOBER

VIII

He died in a desert town. The quiet
of his lines, baking. In the heat, where
something in the trees, is. Rising, as birds
might. I am not there, to interrupt. Or to
cut, irrationally, in. Perhaps I slide my finger
along the edge, each. Blade too close
to see, now. It is autumn. Insist on its
seriousness. This seam, inside frayed.
To pull apart, as threads do, when.
Flesh expands. And darned up, badly,
the lift of matter. Tugs and scabs, not
for want of trying. He runs, awkwardly.
Enough to leave them, sometimes. To
work their own accommodation, each.
Space can be a fragment, a sliver. Of
shrapnel, tossed up. In circumstance.
Dragging on the skin. Or a number of
other things. A stumbling looking after,
he said. Did he, or perhaps not. The time
when soot. Flooded the room, a bird
escaping, when. In the process of relating,
the same event occurred. The time, when
soot had flooded. The astonishment
of friends, at this relation. Clearing up,
after. In every finger, there are. Silences,
drawn along, and rough. Against, what
surfaces. Or lines, when he was here. Not
sparing the impulse, when. What bird falls.

2 OCTOBER

IX

Inconstancies. The flow of water is moving. Uptide
and downriver, all the same. Moment, shunting. Or
is it a frayed rope, needing a warehouse. Long as a
city, and strong arms. Twisting. Trust to machinery,
he does. Leaving notes to himself, a mark of later
incorporation, and you. Need not be too bashful,
speak your mind, or name. Something gives you the
right to speak, what. Can feel like a blaze, half-lit.
Moon brighter, the smoke of the sky. Halo. He said,
what surges in you. Cover your face is a separation,
her eyes are laughing, however. What comes out
of need. Seas dragged up, the test of something
flowing. Is small objects sent under. The river was
a rain, and flew, he wrote. Disturb marks of separation,
challenge them freely, is not. The point, here. Tell me
where you are in all this. Water is pulled along, a skin.
Knotting, where the nerves are. It is high, anticipating
night forces, rising. Send them under, and wait for
reappearance after the bridge. The swimmer on his back,
kicks with white limbs, diagonal. They say your
head is low in the water always. The helix of a water snake
crossing the brown canal requires calm, where. You have
none, and fear. Do not give me money, I may throw
it into. The air, on the bridge. Strange as fortune, or
falling. In muscular water, I lay me down. Rolling,
buoys, barges. If I cross you lose me, but the danger is
transverse. Not stamina, but stanchions, pleasure
boats, cormorants. Collision, a firework suddenly.

7 OCTOBER

17

They want you to be present, to the extent.
Voices call you out, keep you. In motion,
doors, please. The road is motionless, speed
keeps it in check. She says, this. Sound
is by itself, it is no memory. There is pressure
on the eardrums, as if we fell, to think. Otherwise.
A sneeze from another garden, sutures. So how
would you speak it, that gap. When she cries she
fights the air, there are no children here however.
She wrote. The crepiness of skin is an abstract
comfort, though it astonishes. Caught in the window,
who. Is that, not realising. Ferns die back from
the outside. What made her falter, it was what.
Came at her, I think, in words. A body has to work
to keep itself. Alert, but there is somehow abandon.
She has a quiet smile, wonder if people. Come at
each other as transparencies, ghosts, more fragile,
slower. When words are where matter is, also more
lasting. Residue of violence, still recovering. Sh
Shadwell. Machine stutters, ha harbour, take
all your belongings with you. Be be longings. You
would only find that. In England he said, waiting.
His briefcase. Yellow. What would you keep pace
with, knowing. Their use of colour, rose and gem
stones, and strewn bodies, is not pity. Reliquary,
maybe. Is this mine, without principles. Connecting,
a hum, to be cared for. Transport, not easily managed,
but today it is enough, she says. In its measure.

9 October

XI

Already beginning again. Wood splits along
a length, a hammer. Silence preens, as if scarcity
confers. Luckiness, like a spring day it announced.
Building, the sound. Voices, inhabiting. You never
listen, he said, let me. Finish my sentence. What
will they take from this meeting, the memory of.
Cadences, que lindo. Mexico City, splashing
from its cup. When ash falls, the celebration of
blue eyes, fungus on the corn, huitlacoche. But
not the rolling r of ferrocarril. He has a fear of volcanos,
it may dull the pain. Of flying, feel it budding on
his shoulders. Yesterday the river was tame. Warm,
with players out along the banks. Throwing coins at
sand men, the man who was the Mona Lisa, hundreds
waiting to slide. Autumn sends out spores, we all.
Cough and wait for invasion, mist, the cool of
seasons. The trees are dying, it is not natural. Life
congregates, still. Waking up to mass destruction
on the radio, Sunday. Splashing up the hillsides
as far as you can see. From the plane, planetary.
Settling, he laughed. Isn't it always the way.
The breeze with an edge of salt. Horn from distant
boats. Does it run through me, more than. The vision
of the brow of a hill, a hip of land, giving way to.
What comes over will be where I am. Or want to be,
a promise, scenting. Practice will not bring it nearer.
She thinks, do you. Reach out ahead of yourself.
Pharoahcarril, fair ochre reel. Furrow qua real.

15 OCTOBER

XII

A story of breath. Crowds in Spain go.
Hoooooooooooooooooooooooooooooooooooooooooooooooor.
Here they go haaaaaaaaaaaaaaaaaaaaaaaaaaaaaaaaaaaaaaaaaaaaaaaay.
The sound of hot air balloons, climbing close.
When house owners sleep, shaving. The incline
of roofs, ropes trailing. If you held on, where.
Would it lead, in this light, with a last long.
Inflating, his acoustics are keen, quick as a
reflex. Astonishing what they pick up, in a glance.
Apparently, as if language buzzes on your lips.
Geographies in the expelling of air, joy. Chants.
In attitudes of bodies, klaxons. Headline moments.
Today he corrects my hesitant corazon, draws it
with small arteries. Because it is not like that,
indicating. Index fingers, rorschach mirroring.
What it takes to make it beat, sketch
connections. Yesterday the walls were gilt.
The world was shining, the persistence. Of sun
in its decline. When the thought of dying
accompanies, is a sleep. You might choose
sometimes, going to ground. Green ground.
Grass, just beneath the mowing, rest. Some
atonement for a previous shortcoming, is.
Announced. Then, later I heard him say. Fish,
speech. Deciding, duration is to stay around,
hear more, to risk. Without protection, a decision.
Coming from this skin, pulse, the night play of light.
Breath demands, it puts you. Present, massing here.

XIII

At the borders of this do you decide to let go.
Shapes and intimations, perhaps what they mean
is not important. Just an impelling, setting a shoulder
to. The wind, rising the further north you go today.
He covers a lot of deliberate ground, but water
colours it. Pewter, olive. I will tell you what, she says.
Pooling in your hands, as metal does when it falls.
It is a watershed in many directions. Liquid,
the route to the north that came through her lilac
curtains. They swayed at night, and down the rally
we went. It spills differently, from the palm, drains
away. Even when you hope to catch it, and taste.
You could not know that. Waving and counting, they
respond to children in the 1960s. Inside the low whistle
over the Mystic, another order of sound. This summer,
the journey through the reed beds, and no-one seeing.
The clarity, preserving as brine does. Close my eyes
in the blue dress. Scent of fishcutter's house, the noise
when the tide turns. Far inland, walking the bridge
over the mill pond, her tales. Of the blue lagoon,
deafness, near where he built over the tracks, where.
They all built the tracks, moving along them for
work even to France. Where do these lines. Lead,
the taste of water. Shells of oysters, prised, discovering
a palate for live, flinching things. When the knife slits
and then cracks the hinge, scraping. There they sit,
with the same vulnerabilities and embarrassments.
Grit, then a long clear line equal to the freshness of air.

XIV

I think we will be aloud. Passing sentences
of articulated traffic, sheet metal permission.
To deal in trapezoidal bulks, or Floridian
land and reality ventures. At night, illuminated
red squares, processing arterial sequences
where speed tells. Geometry is not my best suit,
having backed into the man with yarmulka.
There is always a first time, he said. So far
from south of the river. Mechanical abandon
is not advisory. Night is granular, an irritant
smoothing you deceptively. One tree hill,
the border of a city, lit from below, catches.
The periphery, where you are. Negative,
a dream of earlier technologies of seeing.
A nitrate needing recovery, you begin
decomposition. Perhaps it will resolve, at
a point to be determined by everyone seriously.
Clocks retreat and it is the end of summer. Time
to store banks of darkness. The sound of fire, fed.
Applewood, cherry, oak, chestnut, ash, beech.
The three day week when they put candles on
the landing. Walls loomed, we depended
on chimneys. She cleaned the grate with a cold
wet cloth, the ember. Stuck to her skin. Spindles
of newsprint helix without unravelling. Coke
saved in the hearth. Radio whispers, foil
frames. St Paul's in the Blitz, Highland stags.
Red, purple. Transformations. Tock. Tock.

28 OCTOBER

XV

The absence of harm is not the place to begin.
In the mildness of. Seasons, insufficient leaf
fall, they hang on. By the last thread, needing.
Definition, the gasp of frost. To let go. I know
what it is and then I do not, this game. Quietens
us down. If you break it open why, is there only
this silence, cracked open, the salt of other.
Pain, is not mine to own. It does not have a
cavity, for light. Or breath, but it serves, pain
persisting. To find a relation. Will you cut out
eyes and mouth, place it. At the window, lamp
for an evening. When they come asking, or
punishing. Replace the roof, it begins to burn.
That is for tomorrow. Now the purl of sky engine,
the point when it turns, sound dropping. Will
descent remain after it has gone, do we. Know
the reliance of gravity as a reluctant measure.
When it leaves us, only. Aggregations, do not
think of it as a lightness. Stacks of crimson,
the gnarl of globes, residues. Of distant earth,
chambers of flesh and light. The nature of over
wintering, buoyed up, hardened to its lasting, is.
Convincing, it does not ask to be. A mode of
attention. The thickness, is a red hide. Density
reassures, the beat of. Knuckles checking
ripeness, you know. He said, the rest are all
sold, and these the last. Red, green veins, will
open at the ceremonial, the knife. Sticks.

31 OCTOBER

XVI

Something of an evacuation of light. Persists,
it knows the ending of day. Approaches, it turns
towards heat as love might. Deep in the earth,
rotting gently, sweat. Of leaves, skin's sudden
exposure. Plane trees, in intentional mottling
effect, sun spots. Ruching, experience. Not
ruins, or rubble, but run. Through, as if will carries
you, burning. Off what you jettison, what springs
in your wake, it is heaviness. Dragging out bones,
the bow of waking minutes, concentrations. Let
go, with leaf fall, and small flakiness, bark. Rills
of stiff. Lace. An hour passes, more. Modulation,
without birds, the clear reach. Where horizon is
imagined. Trees cascade, rust hoards, are coin.
Showers, each picked out by shadows. Each,
tearing holes, round. Puncturing air, she chases
her grandmother's long line, it disappears into.
A cold lack of light, temporary. Respite from glare
of an old sun. She does not need to move much.
She says, take advantage of the day, in a patchwork
coat. It is not a how but a why, he points. Out,
a sense of injustice. It is the way woodsmoke brings
life forward, strong as leather, the way yesterday
always joins. With. Scenting tomorrow, its yellow
haunting. A glow, not without. Loss, anticipated,
as an inhabiting of flesh, a brilliance kept secret.
Known everywhere, in its hiding, he says. Even
describing this tree, is imagination, I have a right.

XVII

Is it so much later. Word from a shouting river.
Arrives, it is the interim. Before an Atlantic
storm, with hours of quiet rising. Weakness,
in light, lays down to rest. The falling out
of purpose. Opportunity to see a sequence, in.
Time, in one, the action starts out like a hunt.
Cut a story short. There he arrives, in the fourth,
and the game is bagged up. Yet, she said, this.
Could never be known, unless you saw them
together. The man who jumped from a tower
and flew a furlong. Wanted movement forward,
it was said. He could have improved on that
performance, if a tail had occurred to him.
But was prevented and lived, ripely. An impelling.
Towards, the risk of arrival. When sky darkens,
in notches, but it is too soon. Birds fall out,
expecting shattering, hold breath. And regroup
soundlessly, the fatigue of alarm silences.
Can we calculate the rising of water, he asks,
in inches. Using measurements handed in, always
the turn of the archaic. As if seriousness comes
that way. Looking at his feet, they already push.
Through the flow, the child stamps. He wrote,
the illusion of facing it well. Is our inhabiting,
handed on. In an impulse for protection, perhaps,
or the other side. Of a rationing, as if the chance
for anticipation remains. Possible light, drifts.
A cat. Descends in three, wall, ledge, sill. Cries.

24 NOVEMBER

2 wintercuts

It is in the nature of light. Where lack is grainy.
Presence, folding over. Imagine it below or above,
lit. Uninterrupted. Or gladly, in excitement, blue.
How many seeds were eaten to keep it shadowed.
Some say six, or three. Paint your houses white,
grow trees by the door. In anticipation of possible
catastrophe we might enjoy, nonetheless. As we
fall. Down, down, nothing falls now. The berries
are gone. Are parakeets silent in the park. She hopes
children might see them, but. He is angry under
a tree in sight of his mother. He is small and water
overwhelms him. He has a red round face. Mouths
open as buds will. They are already hungry for now.
Go away. Cat, it slinks. In a seasonal mottling,
wool is shawled over the afternoon in the manner of
comfort. Speeding clouds, in search of. Do you think
of tincture as medicinal. Not as dilutions of colour.
Gravity. Of rain approaching. We will take a direct
hit. Mid-week, it announces. Legions of water
passing by, stiffness of limbs. Waving vainly, spindle
yarns from it. Past four and still the mocking. Flyes
in mistery winters peace. He wrote before walking,
his feet. Were agony, tiredness came on as a storm
does. Even then. In the darkness clouds become
light, or bring night on. As smoke. Rooms glow,
interior saintliness everywhere. Is there balance.
She saw a bee at the window. She saw a red bagged
bee, its heaviness. Surviving, and pointed it out.

7 JANUARY

||

There are so many things I want to say. She said.
Was she a torrent, flood. Where lines drag, bagged
up. Are buffered, warping. As doors do, held shut.
Shut. Saturate those locks and commas. Is there
escape to learn gamely, while the wind rises.
When shelter is the first rule. Does it turn about
itself, what is it that soughs in cities, the absence
of trees. Sounds of husks, plastic thundering, wails.
Something is built. When the sea draws through
stones, the same is indrawn. If you could add gentian
violet to the wind. She kept purple bottled in.
The cupboard, it stained her stomach. Why did she
paint it on. It would wrap you, the breeze would add
up eventually to darkness, over and over. Wind
makes landfall, its transparency is fortunate. If
suffocation is to be avoided, preferring. Vagueness
in clouds. The way things whip up, unknowing.
Infinitely. What if the forms always arrived to sight,
rampaging. In collections of things, tails, scarves,
trailing arms. Is it her dressing table spilling, piling
down the hillside. Tights, stockings. The flow of
American tan. The rush of her before the mirror.
I broke her compact. Opening a bottle of coca-cola
at midnight. Sweetness without release, the top
stuck, hacked away at. Fizzst. Does she gust through
in powdered mustiness. Unseasonal pollen, paisley
anachronism, the presence of purple was. Never her
colour but returns her now unexpectedly, turbulent.

11 JANUARY

III

Green grass hills. Does she watch from her own
window. First the silos open. Missiles rise
to acclaim and clapping. Of assembled. First they.
And then they descend to deeper levels. In the
green grass hills is the sun shining, happily. It is
not, snow is. Forecast, while others are balmier.
Is there a problem with negotiate. There is not enough
clarity, I do not speak. Well. Then they close, all is
as it was. Small furies hop along the path, nipping
at anything exposed. The prospect seems benign but
other words suggest you are mistaken. Gnaw, is one.
Talk about hard power. Is it in the nature of derivatives
to feel. Such confusion and then posturing, and not.
The soft inhabiting of speech, the point. Where it lifts
and life is, in real. Time, it is the ticking of your skin.
Poverty arises in control of all of this, fear. Of words.
Sweeping, the sheer flirt of seriousness. Is where joy
meets the possibility of. Ending, each time. You open
your mouth. It is all you can do to hold on. On these
occasions, though. Nothing remains for future reference.
Tell me you grasp. Today, the story of. The man who
drew out the word encounter. Drawing it over and over.
Gently, he would sing in Cajun. It is said, on his island,
watching her. Decline. And finally left accompanying
something he could not live. Without, drawing loss.
For others, in the shape of polar bears. When all along
he may have had in mind. Negotiation, its soft inhabiting,
as something total, without more words to say.

12 JANUARY

IV

Is there a binding of insignificant things. Cast in
your direction, they are. Twigs in a stream. Some
thing makes them swerve, it could be chance or.
Unluckiness, to be bound up. Facing inward, as
if falling. Due at a certain time, without prediction.
As cadences arrive. Accidentally, when in future
hindsight nothing. More could have been the case.
As you imagine. Finding messages. Are dry dust
seeds, and you hoarding. Is there later germination
or just safekeeping, for another. Time, is there.
Luxury in thoughts of distant retrospection, when.
Things can be owned, as testimony you were once.
Loved. It said the dears in the park are dangerous,
and. Combine, combine, with small diagrams. Not
meant for me, I wrapped it. Along with a red book
reporting. The parents are caring. And a spidery
note stashed. In a history of corsets, saying your
mother will help you open them. Another, write
back. Where she had reversed it. Fainter, already
it fades. Thinking this is altogether too replete, or
hopeful in its. Recoveries, that you might be. Glad
to know I kept. All of you, safe. Is that too much
holding. To bear, brightness. Made a woman laugh
today. She laughed, imagine. This so early in January,
we all laughed. Sometimes it is the smallest twist,
you would see. Its disturbance, an eyelash. Floated
there, interrupting. The dust is from meteorites, it falls
and we are all thrown. Motes, lit. Collisions, softly.

20 JANUARY

V

Now she has grown older. Does her voice stretch to
high sharps. Thinner and warm, they felt. And
browner than black. The man who spoke of shades
of brown, catching it exactly, he was. Stooping to
talk in. Internal strings and hammers. She played
with stubby fingers, they leapt sometimes. She sings.
Is it almost completion, the sound of. Roundness in
a force of words, chambers you move into. Are organ
pipes, cliff stacks. She sings. Flesh mounts up, volumes
of hot outpouring. Basalt cools in tall columns. Suddenly
there is a great surf, in rooms with distant ceilings.
Every listening ear finds itself inside the crashing. Is the
chance of exchange not quite extinguished. Over there
it burns up as oxygen does, leaving lagoons of lower
water. Thoughts of last breaths rise, heavy and flapping.
And stream downwards. Are they collapsible. Pelicans
carry supplies, but these do not. Breathe in. There is, this
brink. Do we step out in our weight of biology. Or dive
with the minimum of disturbance. Tell me, when she sings
again. If appearance matters, or. Air, what is it that thickens
in us. Out. When she mispronounces, it changes nothing.
It helps to know some German, but I have forgotten, is.
In all languages. Do we imagine it remains, or continues.
She only saw it for the first time. That day, she said,
it was already. Committed. And beating time, you could see
her eyebrows, anticipating. Comes in the form of wrists
and shoulders, the body thinks first, does it. Turning
towards, as a plant might. Without occasion, or event.

24 JANUARY

VI

Snow arrives and then it leaves. White gouts.
Shall I put my tongue in it. No it collects particulars,
in small dark flecks. The wind from the east brings
the scent of bread baking. Or sweet yams or yeast.
Fermenting, then the earth rises. It reclaims intensity,
of everyday things, all. Returning to grey and brown,
wetly. Open your eyes, they told her, and light arrived
electric. It was green and blue, and each branch
had a million droplets shining, she. Had never expected.
There was however disappointment in crowds, she saw
dishevelment on buses, unimagined on a scale. Of detail
suddenly apparent. Would that overwhelm. You know
snow comes with a quietness, it insulates us. From
what is driven, it weaves itself between the keys. Do
we know what is suspended in its falling. Look, he said,
what has happened to us. I was dragged along on a sled
by my father. He was a young man. The same year as the
moon landing, was it. No more than a pinch. Children spin
down the grass hill, on traffic signs. No Entry is fast,
it threatens. Limbs of the unprepared, the illusion of
insulation, there is just. Earth, it sprays and slides, wetly.
So fast, it is a round disc. Cutting without drag, unanimous
yawping. There is the absence of control to think of.
Enough to close your eyes, and bring them down safely.
Screaming, abandon is. A texture to own, it is a headlong.
Freedom, you buffer it. Mistakenly, sometimes, do you
willingly find us corticate, it is a matter for protection.
Are you called out in snow for the briefest hour it arrives.

27 JANUARY

VII

Does it ring, the world. Yes, he said, what should
I write. The words are welding, incredulously and.
Ventriloquist, what is that. I just can't believe/ how
you fused them with angry fire/ the hand said. Or.
Now the sun falls in long yellow planes. And your
feet discover the nature of hills, you cannot see for
the glow. Of equanimity, in that second when. Eyes
are ponds of light, your lashes are reeds, protecting
from. This pain of apertures, while. You extend
in to warmth, guiltily, as something reflected, paved.
Seizes you. It is not a sidewalk. But something fronted,
it. Demands all you have. Letting go, in matters of trust.
The give encountered in streets, you see it in faces,
when they. Sag, fold into themselves. Do you call it
a reverie in so many. We think of it as tiredness, but
it is only thought. And not inward, but called out by.
The same transparent wall of windows when the train
passes at night. Illuminated at uncertain distance.
Opacities of powdered nearness. Heat is a prematurity
in this season, it is sneezed out. Bleated confessionals.
That cross-hatching is the skin of the world, it is
our inhabiting in. The space of a sleepwalker, he
thundered down the stairs unknowing. His hand upon
the door. The woman slept on the jib fifty feet up,
having climbed. With deliberation, do we all climb.
Where it is a matter of joining disparate states and
unlike materials. The shock of this is usefully muffled
yet you do. Come to at this rim, mouth. Spoken.

5 FEBRUARY

VIII

Things fly at night in white leaves, you would
not. See them without vision, he said. With
their fluttering about him. Do doors always
hammer in sleep. Ears make out differences,
the sudden coyness of birds speak them openly.
Did you hear them singing, I banged on the wall.
He said, perhaps he works in the video store.
Do you think I should have. There was indignation,
he carried a blue broom. It was overcast today,
and when the rain fell. The persistence of fingers
came to mind, you could feel them drumming
before water followed. First the fence begins, then
the brick. Until leaves arrive in a wave, they shake
each. Time, before impact, each flinching. Open
anticipations of downpour are reassuring, everyone.
Looks up at the sky, will it come before. Covies
break, where. Masses are incontrovertible. There
are no distinctions between wings and leaves in
the dark. Undersides are silver, they are picked out.
Do you brush them away, when sonar fails and they
abut. Without meaning to, you are a wall sometimes.
The garden extends a breath, it would like to be
longer in the span. Of flying things, leaves bank up.
In the consternation of hedges, are limits of real
estate twittering. Rotting down, the season begins
with the sounds of geese arriving. The fakery of
children. When they alight. Brushing away thought
of a leaf. Was a sharp sting in my palm, distracting.

16 FEBRUARY

IX

Are there hidden features. Reluctantly given
up for fear of higher pricing. Conflict exposes
the shape of chimneys, some can pick them out
instantly. Space gives way to sky in all cases.
Composing is a ratcheting of desires, finds
permutations, it is all you can manage to be.
Quiet. The word listening is a metaphor, but we
do need to learn it, sometimes look at me when
you speak. Today there was a gap between fronts,
and clouds were reflective. The sea broke over.
The bar, it was grey where the river ran out.
Behind eyelids red rapids bloom, slowing down
until calm. Steadies, nightfall. Bodies stretch on
small pullies, do they think in stretching. Like that,
she would have said, her spine is a helix. Rocking,
or suddenly thrown. What is lived in spaces beyond
mutedness. When light is enough, and a chair.
Is there more to be had than this. Memorializing
chokes up, standing in for. Lives, where endlessness
is. Tax deductible, more than the right of children.
Only, tell them to grow up. This is all there is,
not smooth fantasies of reckoning, just blood where
it beats and stops. He reaches to shake that hand
but he would end its pulsing sure. As mine ticks
over, now all he says is look. Feel my heartfelt.
Belief in the heat of decisions. Interests in higher
causes make him sweat fervently. We are all costed,
sound gongs, appeasings, hear the beating. Stop.

21 FEBRUARY

Seagulls suspend, are thought against the bridge.
In the red light, are they. Original, or shadows
where the footpath led to crossings. Reconstructed
in the desert. Do we still cross in the rain on dark
evenings. There are small passages. Thought takes.
Place, it retreats. In speed and roaring, the clacking
of heels. There is deliberation in umbrellas from moment
to. Are trumpet stops, pumping. Is goodwill always
resentful here, at root. Fed in the largeness of crowds,
headless, cowed by. The city is really a tar pit at night,
it mires you. In that black gleam, feet up. Faces are
temporary, grease. On window glass, or globs of wax
shed from some source of light. They don't stay around,
are lunar phases, rinds. Of preoccupation, do they look.
Up, glances ring from deeper buried bells, foundries and
inclines, Ludgate. Hill, birds find it extended upward.
Necks and knees fix stiffly, where. There is only chance
to move forward, in the measuring of geometries,
some disturbance troubles connection. It is a graph badly
drawn, where a free hand misses the meeting of a line.
No-one is relaxed about this. Do take heart, in cities,
from inconsequence in rainy homecomings. Matter rises,
boxes in church doors mount in Bow Lane. He sleeps
lit and hooded by overlooking absence, where they
did cross once, you are tempted to say pilgrims wrongly.
The river is catgut, it twists and knots, there are
patches of sheen. What dives for many minutes. Tiredness
in infinite register, muscular ligaments of. Ancient footfall.

3 MARCH

XI

The first time for six years she announces, peaking
now. Spectrum of light extracts everything lunar.
As if fierceness gives way to. Planetary etiquette,
larger peacefulness in scale. He said the moon is a
plum, take a. Picture requiring steadiness, how much
we all tremble, unknowing. Exposure is slow, the shutter
pulls and shunts, your heart is in your palm. It delays
the way fear interrupts. Turns out, captures a white bead,
where red light is rushing in. For hours. Did they all
live in the hush of lanterns. Imagine the constancy of
local faces is. Our indulgence, they leached away in the
dark, it is electricity and not the sun providing. A contrast,
he composing from coal and broccoli the rocks and trees.
In winter evenings, needing objects. Firelight is your
addition, this scent of ash. He would save logs for knots
and hollows, thought. Of what hands might do if they.
Could make the time, spit embers. Burning close by,
this very ten minutes before. Twelve, I sleep. Riding
on what is blotting out, soaking up, the roundness of its
intervention is. Reassurance, even then it can feel. This
fast and spinning. Do we interrupt the sun too often for
health in dreaming. Nights ago I saw a bauxite plant,
the heat of midday on an orange beach. With silver
pipes for. Chimneys, the sand. Was orange because of
minerals, the rocks. Were smooth. Pink, micas. In the bay
the sharks could not be seen. We are protected by nets
and buoys. They said, it was unconvincing on the reef.
How does a sphere move us in sleeping and waking.

4 MARCH

XII

Wind sounds off, then it ransacks. Does it move
around to the left or the right in this hemisphere.
Water slowly lets itself go in this house. But the
door bursts, the weakness of locks is a reminder.
That wills itself to dilate internally, it opens planes
and walls. All at once are words beating. At the
window, the slap. Of rain, hell for leather cats.
Come home, after days of looking, locked away.
The wind is too much to bear. For creatures, does
the eucalyptus bend, it shivers and whips. Birds
and clocks have a counterbalance, but others spring
about colliding when. Machinery descends, do we
stand under lintels in our minds. Do we, stand.
Under lintels. Anywhere. Walking on the surface
of snow requires outlay, a willingness to leak beyond
confines. Of body mass, in conditions of curvature,
so that planetary dimensions are. They are to be
defining in these cases. Yet absent in wind and rain
where bodies are molecular, they. Salt down into
conditions or stream away, he said osmosis is not
the right word. Absorb, would suggest. Membranes
when they work in one direction only. When drawn
by tides, are bodies just taking up elements, or
dissolving. As small tongues and rills of skin
slough off into the next downpour, whorls and
imprints, corpuscular breezes, and lashes of.
Are wound up, and wind. Or bed down, are what
we stand on and splash through, are what lift also.

10 March

40

XIII

Do they drum insistently at intersections, always.
The same place, with fanfares. Weaving through,
and inside. Are they worn so everything is exposed.
Ribs and entrails, lines of. Pain turned acoustic
witnessing. Zoom zoom has lightness about it, but.
So, where. They had left them with small tokens was
still rending. One had left a hazelnut with her baby.
But anonymity was prized, so she remained. Lost to
herself, in the cabinet. It was lived as are natural
gifts. His was mother of pearl with Jamaica inscribed
unsteadily. Did they wear organs on the outside. Weeping
for, infants. Is a condition often arriving later. Inner
banshees. Don't drag me, she wailed in the supermarket.
If truth is possible in congregations. Its intervals
this homecoming were reliable, stacking up in the sky.
Where the grey clouds were filings, drifts of. Lambs,
wool caught on barbs when. Seasons turn, green comes
almost. As future's afterthought, when it can. Is there
honesty in expanses, if you stay with them, or. Do they
stare blankly, when truly confronted. The group of boys
throwing cans at passing strangers were only boys. A
sentence to travel through, slowly. He reassured me
that his fiery red hands might strike back offensively.
Blunt fragments of ice were also possible avenues.
Sometimes anxiety blossoms white magnolias, we are
sick of that. Scent without accompanying greenery.
We get the bones under the sap this week, the woman
said. History put her off her food, from Romans to WW2.

10 MARCH

XIV

First day with doors open, the cool sun. Turns
dust and stains to viral sections, shone through.
Must wipe clean, sight relies on housekeeping.
The drone is languorous, it knows the language
will come into conformity with time, and possible
heat. What is a slut, he asked yesterday, seeing.
Barbie is one. I would not wear it. There is excess
in the air, it comes from taking things too earnestly.
That is what happens when. Discipline occurs.
Too many words bring shame and embarrassment,
is that why. No-one speaks to name where we are.
Or how faces always look away, without. Trying
out other faculties, that unintelligible ear. Do we all
prefer the neatness of violence, here, since we mete it
out, with the benefit of future. Hindsight, if only we had.
Known, that. Or, yes. Enjoy this culpability and then.
There is no imagining otherwise, even when spring is
indulgent. Someone is weakly whistling the second
verse. The times they are a, again. Scraping. While he
clears the moss away from dark flagstones, leaf
mould. Stains the stars of veins crimson, imprinted.
It is a Sunday, this one. Begins the next phase of.
The year, so convalescence is over, you need to try.
Out your new eyes with bandages unwound. First
there is that lightening around your temples, then you.
Feel that scurviness of skin, itching in warm beams
of. Lids find focal points, they do have vanishing
to contend with, it may be the world or you seeing.

11 MARCH

XV

Measure the size of adequate things, where. The eye
flies off in uniformity, where. Expected symmetry
regroups. Were we here all along, she said, did she
muse. Often, out in the bathhouse and the giant mangle
turning sheets. Enough strength it took, steam. Blanch,
would skin your fingers. Were we married to industrial
patterns, the cutouts of shoes. Sown in the alley, then no
more. Go/don't go is an instrument, tests ranges of deviancy,
what fit. Arrives with machines, when labour is required,
to bring them into line, the promise of reproducibility.
When now. Beyond labour, we are impossibly synchronous
with ourselves. She would not know me. Did not know
the nature of rest, more human in its drive than. Driven
children can ever know, the sorrow of infinite calibration
endlessly. Descending, as kites do. Tipping towards the
ground, the rush. Of frames, their poleaxing has a violent.
Intent, it knows prohibition slams into play, the love
of control. Is our great love, is it. A fall gives way to
prodigious learning. Or its occasion. Are we all better
for the lesson. Stop, she said, look under the lid. The sand
was damp, she had. Had she engineered a small space
in the yard. In the darkness there was manoeuvring of limbs.
Sometimes retreat, the trick was. To snatch it high over your
head, to go for full exposure in the light. So that you were
the conditions of horizon, its world's end. Able to find it at
will, looking down. Was there thunder in its ears, the glint
of yellow iris. Brought from a husband's garden, had she.
Thought that consistency. Trapped, its copper eyes.

14 MARCH

XVI

Small insistencies build, they are. Accusations
occasionally, weighing more than houses. Is that
why. She ended, since she was her own reminder.
I recall, she wrote. And then, I recall. When no-one could
move beyond that beginning. To grant the opportunity
of returns, the shift of a typewriter is already. Archaic,
emphasis remains in how things are shouldered. Among
certain gestures, bells ring. Also the fear of undoing
shifts us, or it is arresting. Stands in for. Experience,
do we turn our back on. Repetition, it scores the ground
each time it passes by, the swish of. Just cutting the firm
ground neater. Patches of turf rolled up and ready.
Each thirty seconds. Each thirty seconds for want of.
A net, each thirty seconds a child. Is it *now*. Each thirty.
Seconds. Has not been prevented, we do not. Prevent.
No I do not prevent the return. Each thirty seconds,
without a net. Of endings, she was accused. I recall.
This is green. These are patches of clover, perhaps.
There is drumming. In that timber, on a warm day.
Does it repeat only. Or in conjunction. With unseen
lines, the spider shoots. Silk upward, catching. Nothing
familiar. And light, bearing itself towards. This margin.
There is rustling, the cat. Takes time to walk the plank,
choosing to avoid the cracks. The long backbone flows.
Is a wave in the breeze, sending out eddies, or. Just
haze, as heat will. In insufficient clarity, but here.
Definition is only troubled by the rubble of looking,
it has clean lines by itself, is green even in shadows.

28 MARCH

XVII

Do the deer move by slowly in the garden. In
layers, where green is discriminating. Appearing
and not appearing, where they do not return to see
who is watching. Two birds are paper curls, burnt
off, and then five. There is foreign commotion.
Sometimes mobbing is airborne, requiring noise,
where exhaustion quickly follows. The point is.
Made in succession, duration finds. Pockets of reserve
in fewer words. What is it that fades, the rim of
winter seen off. Does it retreat or send out. Emissaries,
in fungal lines running under. The stones, the mud
shales with small blow holes. Made by. Older air,
broken open to sighs and cracking. Not in relief, not
resignation either, but in occasions. Caught up,
broken out, in the same instance as a rose bush
budding by the window. Among lost roses, sprays
and geological moments marking. The stone from
the beach. Is a golden knuckle, it sits also by the
window. Among amber bees who may be outside,
though they. Sit in the sun, and pulse gently today.
Bark strips down, there is a blonder mottling, and
grey wintergreen. You could chew, it would take
you into spring safely, if your constitution allowed.
This, is acknowledging. Where earth might be built
up, quietly, alongside. The sliding of greater faults,
in pieces, for the growing of snow peas. Fruit will,
where land hangs. A pendulum wrapped in a web.
Struggles, is buffered, until weight gives way.

29 MARCH

3 springcuts

|

Rest, is. Also a gathering. Sometimes,
it constellates happily, or pintucks. Tacked
up for later attention, in. Moments of early
afternoon, when labour is. Required, there
are. Patches of quiet worked in, pulled down
where thought. Waits in deeper compass,
it waits. Awhile. For the clearing of ground
to end, when gleaning is. A later gathering
that stacks up hopefully. Later corn will grow
as high as the fence, does it. Begin in thought
before ground determines. Where it rises,
already. Where birds quilt *in* sound, when
they prick it out in shoots. Or in small pursed
seeds. Bursting. Are there cries. Of alarm at
beginning again, or. Nothing of contention,
just round in the palm repeatedly. Watered
to the depth of several minutes. Do they answer,
each. Hole is an undertaking, a wager with.
The darkness of woods, where. Eyes roll in
the silence, without animals, do they. Return
from broken trees, the blue branches, suddenly.
In spans of limbs and elbows, when waking
is a condition loosely remembered. This tree
bends, it is a woman's back today, it pauses.
Under the moss, aching in hollows. Has the
calendar passed by, or does it fan out. Overhead,
and wheel with others. Congregating, does
it wheel freely. This is. A branch, a root.

II

Tell me it returns, the soughing. Of
deliberate rivulets, the construction
of sluices. Sinking, the heaviest stones,
rolling. The chance of prospecting a.
Gold rush, do they glint. In deposits,
rolling, slower at the base. A small girl
trips along, her mind would be elsewhere.
The drains are overcome, the hill washes.
Where culverts might once, now it is.
Matter. For survival, the overcoming
of life wells from. Below, whatever tidal
surge above. Astonishes, the nature of.
Coastal cities, it is rain recalling us to.
Water. Plaits, it drives down the kerb,
finds. Welcoming estuaries adjoining,
banks of leaves and stones queueing to.
Remember the cheerfulness of erosion,
the incline. Of latent land, as sand mine,
glacial outwash, chalk pit. Might send
out currents, or cut. Through the tarmac,
lifting. The time they tarred over the road
in the rain, it swelled and took the pavement.
Upending, shops and people, all waiting. For
grand eruption, chip shop papers racing,
this birth of a hill. Gleaming black boil,
rising. It rose, until rainwater. Lanced it,
everyone distracted by dogs rutting on the
green as if excitement demanded them.

27 MAY

III

It has not reached. The north, the green.
Creeps as far as it can, but begins earlier.
Some hibernate and appear intermittently
enough. To throw you off. He says this.
Is the case on cold days. An illusion of.
Warmth draws you out, flitting. Until
surprise hits, there is a possible frost.
Retreating, I said. Today we can go inside
a cloud. So you will remember we did.
This, and both looked. To see which one
might be a candidate. How climbing proves
a mechanical prospect. Thought of breath
and lunar cities intervened. Until we did
enter, and were obscured. Queueing to be.
Let in, watching children collide with.
Glass, the blind walking and delight. Where
nearness was. Beyond intuition and body
warmth, with arms. Flailing, somehow
flinging everyone to the margins. The cloud
is loneliness at the centre, sound. Recedes,
with an intimation of crowds escaping. At
the earliest chance. Stumbling in haloes.
Vapour on the eyelashes, dampness. Of
canvas shoes and no-one prepared. When
it comes, there is a rush. Of cool air, it is.
A relief, the billows float boxed. And they
are free, as if you are already behind them,
while. Light is constant, milk-white, home.

29 MAY

IV

Nothing will have taken place. No
one is lost, the sound. Of blackbirds
scattering, still. The loss of summers.
Is refused in that scattering, at night.
Curtains close over the sun, it is high.
Grass yellows, children listen in. Where
the ringing of talk ricochets, the spray
of water, imagined clink. Of glasses,
the supply of adulthood must be. Limitless.
They consider, surely saving up. All those
desires for later. Satiation, what joy must
be. Possible, perhaps. Abroad, or to music.
And now, here. The glow of brick stores
honey for what comes, this side of arrival.
The cleat cleat of parakeets, they dive.
When climate suddenly delivers, genetic.
Memories, the warmth on green feathers
spreads, the cries. Of distant. Calling,
screeing of swifts, piling over. Sycamores,
so many green bunches of keys, floating.
Might unlock depth, is it now. That seasons
give way to density, will they. Flow,
as they did, once. On another scale,
dropping. Wax, the way it cools, skin.
Rucking into something monumental later.
Streams, in the song of. Birds gathering.
Slows towards. Evening, it is the same.
As it was, escaping, to sit. On warm earth.

2 JUNE

V

Flight, is brown. Heaviness rising, as
much commotion as a gesture. Contains,
flung and squawking. Attention, it can.
Be a trial, to others. In the nature of this.
Bystanding, who witness. Such deliberate
pitching, of feathers as. A springing into.
Faces provocatively, when decoys. Are
cheaper and more modest. Fledging is
however. The point where the brink. Is.
Teetering, with much beating. Of wings,
clinging on with delicate. Claws, to any
available nest. It beetles over quite
vertiginously. Will it fall. Has turned into
a swallow, such luck. She said, and not
that heavier. Deal, rib cage consternation.
Where wings hardly lift off. To that
distant parapet. Where the man tending.
Flox, discovering eggs in his windowbox.
Was somewhat astonished, finding. Her
camped out. What will happen, he asked.
When all her offspring need water. Trust
spring to bring it home. To roost, she had
floundered. Tail feathers tossing off.
Down, fluff, juvenile ephemera, puffed.
Out with the breeze, descending. Slowly,
the snow of organisms in deepest oceans
filtered by. Baleines, bottom feeders, her
ballast. Let fly, for some swallow turning.

VI

Running on, in heads, disturbs.
Always. Consequent astonishment,
when it stops. Among the dunes, a
sharpness of. Green whipgrass, cuts.
A possibility, and children charge.
Up, piling down local mesas, limbs
combusting thoughtlessly, flung
faster. Than the sand allows, they
find themselves abrupt. As matter is.
Cooling, in the darkness of. Dug down.
Out of the wind, the cliff is matted.
Heat, the breeze has not caught on.
It is bright, it does not. Court the
earth, things still push through, yet.
Cleanly, where frost might. So it
lifts. Chattering of flesh, uncertain
cauterising in. The blast of sunlight.
Already the lagoon is. Forming,
the tide has a preoccupation, with.
Work, it is going about its. Banks
and elevations, suddenly. From this
shore, ignoring anything decorative.
In air disturbances, or ribbons greener.
Than spring, transversal. Rivulets,
where the sand browns, or is the
cartilege of. Distant estuaries, repeated.
On the soles of feet, later shoes fill with.
Dunes, it is impossible to walk freely.

18 JUNE

VII

No small sums arriving. Or predicted
downpours, days. In the waiting, with
cancellations. Anticipating, where
floods may. The rush of surface area is.
A wave, it is a volume. Without belief,
descending, as all weather. Once, must
have always intimated, in the movement
of. Animals, or the sweat of skin and
instruments. Intimate prediction, left.
To practiced recognition, a word for.
Feeling, ready for accident. Encounter
a swell, pressure in the. Or is it the flush
of systems tracking. Across a lower belt
of Atlantical, hip height. Unusually.
Water trickles through mains and courses,
suggesting. Somewhere, forecasts are.
Achieving trust in general populations.
Will it rain, tomorrow, he is not too
interested. Yes it does, it sets in, a cue.
For rest, the ending of spring, where
growth, the event, sends feelers along a.
Limit, burgeoning. Tut tut under her
breath, you did not control that knotweed.
In time, it is tumescent. Pink, three feet.
Shooting overnight, spray it with b-movie
eradicating pesticide devices. Taking out
everything else in a slight breeze. Rain
removes necessity, *ha*. It comes in harder.

24 JUNE

VIII

Sounds of visible. Movement forward,
are not within earshot. Just plumes of air.
Traffic arc. Of sirens, the chance to.
Find a patch of. Of quiet. Is repetition
over sewn, blanket edged, like I could do.
Insistencies of doors, then they. Come
back the other way. Perhaps it is not
a movement forward. Flickflacking, more,
that events simply repeat. Repeat on
hinges, reversals in each moment.
Unstitching, time. You think you have it.
Taped, then it returns and you see. Your
self, approaching. Unconscious, a deer
in the undergrowth, or embarrassed at.
Meeting, didn't you just come by the other.
Other way, she might say, you. Answer, yes.
Are you caught out by each. But time goes,
it does not unpick from. Skin is older,
readying to crepe up behind you. Meeting
the seconds returning, they were so tired,
children. At a tournament, run out and
flushed, drinking water from paper towels,
they came back quite dejected. Only to
flow the other way, plump with the season.
And you waving them off, have a good.
Day, what you will achieve. By nightfall.
Nothing to stop them backing up, when.
Least expecting it, without ceremonies.

IX

Torrents and numbered bones. Walk
the heath, the same route, unmarked.
Roads, he said. Widened to half a mile
across. The encroachments of feet,
and mules. And ruts from carriages, in
winter. Pushing journeys outwards, to
margins. Which would become the road.
Is a band around the earth holding.
Movement in, how we all do travel still.
Unknowingly perhaps, assumption of.
How generosity comes with land, that.
Is mistaken, it never did, even. Then he
Slept in hedgerows, ate the grass, asking.
Passersby, his feet hurt. He dreamed of
his lost woman waiting. There and that
he was famous, words to conjure with.
Belonged. To another, walking, noting.
A distant rim, glad of a pint, finding sleep.
On a grey day, torrents are expected, but.
It is calm, and older. Thoughts of rinds,
cut around. Pressed out shapes of shoes.
Are absences, the strips of soles along.
Alleyways. They did not add up to. Some
thing, collected. Troubling, to eyes of a.
Child, pulled together in sheaves, scattered.
Leavings, black shreds tending to. Machine
geometries, hands under the lathe, pushed.
Where hands emerge, in making jeopardy.

30 JUNE

X

Spores and seeds. Whirling, colonies of.
Toadstools sucking deadened tree roots,
are. Ganglions in. Invisible skin routs,
the drag of. What it takes, for an organism
to move, when. Time takes hold, in weight.
The pull of summer on that nerve by your.
Mouth, twitching as pain does. Again, the
small stroke of seasons. Watch by the glass
to check for signs. You did not say, she said.
As something rueful, but. Hold on to silence,
its necessity when all is burgeoning, it is.
Extravagant, the green, and lime flowers
sending. Such perfumed fullness out
unnoticed. Skeins and shoelaces from sweet.
Chestnuts, children pack their potion. In
a bottle, grass, water, feathers. Shaken,
brown as a spring would be, if you. Imagine.
When rain comes, percolating. Air drops
coolly, each time it approaches. Then
expands, heat is an action on. Pores, colour
rising from everything where abandonment
is. The condition of life, elasticity loosening.
Definition, cells bursting out of. Systems,
the cartilage. Holding it all down discretely
seems to have. Peeled away, or masticated
and tasteless is spat out in the gutter.
Clearing the airways, how. Do. We take
the exposure. Of seasonal graces.

1 JULY

XI

An equivocal generation. Is a
generation and no generation.
He said, and that his talent was.
A punching of impressions on
words, bringing birds and
animals into alliances with.
Propositions, making moulds.
From his memory of books, in
a time of incarceration. Voyages
among stars and finding truths
in the horizontal moon. That
he might name, and it was.
The nature of constituent life,
finding toads in the heart of.
Rocks, or no. Height in which
there are not flowers, and every.
Word has its marrow in an.
Ear so acute it stings again.
Frost was damp air candied.
To its best advantage, dreaming.
Not of one solution but many.
Sparks flew upwards. Hinging
a Golden Wingged Flycatcher with
some that have the power of
sentences. On a rare thirteenth of
March 1761, prophesies of speckled.
Doves and tigers, no knowing. Of
times and seasons, his chronology.

3 JULY

XII

Metal on the tongue. Is a sliding away
from, when. Days might promise.
Salt licks, ease of congregation rather.
Quarries of clear water, the mildness
of trust in surfaces. Lie with the boatmen,
their impossible angles knowing. Skin
is tensile even when. And can take your
weakness of limbs. Is a sliding away of,
sight feeling. It is not the way forward.
While every sense vantage retreats, into
burrs of. Taste is all that remains. Talk of
layers of security, preventing. Talk of
serpentine roads, made of burnt stones,
uncovered suddenly in. Industrial estates.
The burial of matter, rising. And running
off, causing miscarriages in cattle without.
Recourse to. Justice in water courses, and.
The routes to it, the ignoring of compounds.
As investment in. Possible futures, not for
the living. Molecular, is returned as warfare
in pockets. Where animals and humans
graze knowingly, swim on hot days. Or
in times of deluge, as this last week. With
roots of barley given to. Underwater rice
conversion. Prices shoot for everyone, do
we all pay. Just for quiet and the sough of.
Something like nature, which is a name for.
Retreat, among those who can afford it.

4 JULY

XIII

Is that all. You have to say. When
voices are dark from open windows,
they. Have been tending flowers,
in the sun. Yesterday, the chance
of sky expanded, he was on his knees.
The cherry tree is full, picked off
sourly. Milling under pale berries.
All you have to say to me. A woman
is speaking, where pain is. Domestic
it comes in shades of eavesdropped.
Lack, of light. Gentle murmur, it
transmits, it is a cut in. Credulous,
after all this time. A layer stripped off,
the crust of. Dry webbed. Bark comes
away, in dry seasons, it strews. Where
people walk in quiet forests, building.
A bed, the bands of sun beaming dust.
Torches, grading heat until. Earth is
receptive. Does she feel. This lack, or.
This morning, was it astonishment.
Shining through an open. Window,
mistaken recognitions are. Ordinary,
lattice work. Through which time takes.
Place, the dull kick of resignation has.
Arrived, is celebrated as annunciation.
Of which no-one speaks, happily. They
have a large car. They live on the hill.
Took off his shirt to grow a bed. Irises.

8 JULY

XIV

When the year gave way. To deserted
farms, the tall poplars. Bent, there was.
A bluff. Where a river should have. But
it never was, only in dreams. Remembered
concrete bases, of imaginary pylons. And
something in spate around. Us, never to
be repeated. When journeying around
England. At any point, they would swing
on long ropes, and land on rafters. This
was not a dream, since. Under that bluff
a building. Remained, and it did. Until
1971 perhaps. When poplars shivered
and came down. With a parcelling out of.
Surveyors' sticks, the ice in foundation
holes. Stamped out. In spring, clouds are.
Carriers of changing. Intentions, speeding
in massifs. Never noticed, then, though
the day we did. They threw stones at her,
while. We wondered which one was heaven.
Loyalties, I was silent but. This was virtue,
to stick by in a stoning. Stop. Do you want to.
Be in my gang. Make the sound of an owl
under my window. Her sister was without.
Principles, she had a look of. Faded
Dietrich, and was. Cruel, when entrusted.
We pleaded. Not her. Walking in Spring
Gardens. That day, they threw stones, she
seemed brave, there was a scar on her lip.

8 JULY

XV

Thunder follows. The rip of water,
chasing. Thought of estuaries, then
turning on itself. Wind works smaller
disturbances, out. Sourcing. Everyone
speeds up, colours start to break, strip.
Clean, grey refuses that slate surfacing
it does well against buildings. Slats of.
Monoliths, are. Too bilious sometimes.
To accept, in crowds they. Lord over,
crash, pellets fly down in gobs, catch.
Bare legs, sting perhaps, before. Nothing
remains distinctly, rampaging going on.
At a height, then forgotten. In the rush.
Towards. Light, and blue swathes, you do
congratulate everyone prematurely. It
follows, rucking around, turning on.
Switches, there is rising. In barometric
gorges, a flush of. Damp mounting on
the skin, breath blown from hot throats
somewhere. On the back of a hand. To
check vital heaving in city bodies. This
rain aims to soak evenly. It is no release.
But a pause, in forward. Impulsions, in.
Stacks of. Disturbances, administrating.
So much loudness, birds adapt, raid
brief tongue incursions. Sheltering, from.
Battery, then they dart in open. Dares,
how many. Sound, bound, soar more.

10 JULY

XVI

White sky. Green door flaps,
waits for demolition. S E B 1872,
drawn with a stick, is not official.
It is neighbourly, there is a gable.
Rumours of previous inhabiting
suggest farriers. Or servitude to
greater buildings. It tucks against.
Summer, soon, in brick quietness.
London overspill. Were they red.
Time burns them off. Crusts of soot
are. Air, descending over decades.
He saw the garden from his bed.
Without medication, see the trees.
The making of bricks takes place in.
Sleep, as a firing. Will you bring him
ice. The dip in the sheets is where he.
Was. Purple flowers are extravagant,
go off. In fireworks, they anticipate.
An ending, do they. Bolt already, rust.
Prising from the mortar, roots are
persistent. When unchecked, dig
down. Seeds spray from birds, they
have a stake in selection. Falling among
the cracks, depending on. Size of
beaks, or the darkness. Of feathers and
maturity. White sky browns, it rolls
over towards lunchtime. Once the walls
were higher. Reach the pale tide mark.

10 JULY

XVII

Life exacts. Clack clack heels,
on these. Stone steps, laughing.
And at the same time, he is.
A counterpoint. *ck ck ck*. Angry
to some distant ear. Gesticulates,
you are not in the frame. Do you
stand back, is there courage or.
Retreat in simultaneity. Late
evening light, it does bathe pinkly.
Loving rest, the switch into. Small
bird picked out, wings in a fan.
Now it is loved, by the promise of.
Depth, it is brown. Not at risk.
Gaudier ones are susceptible to
radiation, they. Say you are loved.
Say environments are turbulent,
you. Just don't see them moving,
all those small deaths. On islands
scattered with. Comes from joy, it
carries judgement. Everything does.
At a cost, was there ever. Serenity
in weather patterns, you might own.
Hills rise under your feet, smooth
out. The stagger, do you love. Each
step, taking it in to. Meet refusal of
confines, in one slow breath. They
have gone, and your choreography
with them. Climb. As if arriving.

12 JULY

4 summercuts

Thinking to greet light early. When sun rises,
it falls through the slats in patches. In which
direction to catch it. Surely, the small moth.
Spreads itself on the white wall. Today,
does it sweat. Or take heat from the damp
air, some principle of silicate. Animates,
it has. A brown perfection, scaled from. A
forest floor. Water would recoil, it holds
itself distinct. Will it break, so much mounts.
Skywards, thickened thrown. But held in
vapour, you could not keep it at bay. Unless
something in you. Demanded that desiccation,
in lieu of. Attention. While your mind busies
itself. With elsewhere, and seasons take place.
In a grand rolling, you think. Of extension,
arms outflung, languorous, the weight of
gravity. As resettlement, still. It is night, they
fall over the edge. Are sighing, the sheen of.
Sleep, this dark syrup. Muttering. Bats wildly
against the light, it wheels, is white. Blinding,
so close to. Magnesium flares, the dry roar
of it. On a smaller. But it would seem a
conflagration. Under glass, is that abandon. In
wheeling, or what distraction is. Compulsion
to bring bodies near. Sight, its reach, or. This
trust falling towards. Experience, night secrecies.
Ending. The warm plane of outside, enters.

17 July

II

What did *this* become. Today, large
wheeling cobweb, loose air. Parcels,
striations of midwestern. States, not
strip units, medieval land. Sites, stretched
in unrelenting yellow. Inner working,
crossed in careful round quilting, this.
Window. Glass, counter graphy. Do
layers of clouds hint at currents, she said,
I always. Go there before sleep. And now
here, the guilt of. Convection, rising anvils,
without. Accompanying her at that age.
Small moth has gone. Waves of creepers
descend, unchecked. Filaments shine,
are guy ropes suddenly. For stumbling
weightiness is anticipated, at midday.
Insistent hammers rest unpredictably.
No residue of silence, not precipitate
either. Undergrowth is dark green, to
be hacked. Away, in the deep of houses.
Quiet, so many shrines to. Absence in a
thought of rest. How many hide behind
walls. Hoping to. Discover home silently,
themselves as more than. A remainder
in the ticking out of minutes. I am a coiled
spring, she. Writes, unable to bear. This
estrangement, where energies settle in. To
forgotten elasticity, the slackness of.
Muscles, the way that living turns, waits.

18 JULY

III

Is it a last day of childhood. Declaring he will
count it down, you do not. Own me. Rehearsing
in sleep, predicting. Everything, feeling *that*.
Potent, the span of shoulders. My flower boy,
she wrote. And he kept them safe for her, not.
Knowing when. A child's nape of the neck.
Hiding in the pews, they knelt unexpectedly.
Why do they. His hands were round and hot,
holding on to sleeves. Always, or handles.
Now the sky has cleared for you. It is blue
and racing. Something thunderous expected,
it did hit at midday sulphurously. Torrents
of white falling, ribbons. Drummed up, your
tickertape plummets from providential rolling.
Will you let it spread out. Will it be blithe as
only you manage. Letting it pass with a shrug,
all those centuries. I was in earnest or I was.
Nothing, he wrote, as if friendship fell short of.
Hedgerows and hopes, it is a vivid spark. In
His nature, you bear something. Like, fortitude.
Joy of limbs and dancing, the mystery of.
Number, concatenations of the universe to make
wit from. Are your birthright. Counting every
leaf, on every tree in the road to the next. Directing
how you might respond. In imagined conversing.
Rising to the sunny skin of you, the endless damage
of what the world is. Intuited, stepping up with.
All that brave, lung tempering, sheerness of light.

20 JULY

IV

But the wash of mourning. As it turns. Proves
the world, taps it out. Hollow at the base.
Has the shape of a loaf, it rings dully. If
you fake it, everyone becomes hungry. When
it came down in curtains, I wondered. Did she
know rain, in those last years. Push up that
window, or. Last night there was too much
singing, it was. Enough to push it down, the
sash stuck. Violins under the. Voices took on
loudness, blushing, steam rose as the sun.
Might. Had it not been evening, and Venus
stationary for an instant. Tap it out with knuckles,
estimate. You knead well, nothing left in the
bowl. The oven is not working, not for over a
year. Is there something you have forgotten to.
Add, your inheritance is. Waiting patiently, it
comes to those who. Try all options, whether
they want it, or. Tap it out in familiar signals,
you will recognise I am not a stranger. By the
way, I do it. Technically there is time. For it
to cool down, but we always ate it. Hot, the
knife is useless then, but the scent. Is what
keeps us all interested, it lasted a matter of.
Minutes, there was the one time I ate a whole.
And she laughed and laughed, there was one
slice. Remaining in the outhouse, a gesture.
Of regret, acknowledgement of more to feed.
Nothing, she said, to fill us up, now, nothing.

21 JULY

V

Night, it flicks at the window. Lozenges
of interior glowing. On the hillside tall
houses, make out the internal doors. Could
be a hanging plant or black glass, grand.
Chandelier, moves in the breeze, this. Tree
branch. Dropping crystal in the shadow.
Priced out, no-one can afford even. Mistaken
associations, always. Outbid, the taste of.
Liquorice, called black jacks, did we not.
Realise what that was, preferring. Squares
of fruit salad, and the tall glass jars. Can't
see the face of the man ladling it out. Into
paper twists. Step through, or was it down.
Step down. In summer, going over. On the
railings, taste of iron on the palm. Hanging
with hair reaching the dust. On that morning
she laid out the table. Silverware, it was
disconcerting, knowing which. Was. Sugar,
in such refinement chose wrongly. Spooning
salt over the breakfast, eating every damn
mouthful. While they watched. And puked
it up at school, so as. To hide. My mistake,
unworldiness. Down river, in the warehouse.
Rats in the cherries everyone said. Refining
was industrial, it would flow sometimes
for days. She would buy the tall packets
and see the town written there. Would it be
different now. Spitting out, or still taking more.

21 JULY

VI

Folds of webs are a buffering in light.
Where skin is tessellated. Softness, it
takes. Warmth, gratefully. Can you rest.
Open rose shadows behind your eyelids.
Bloom. In contours, bodies lag naturally.
Speech shapes in another. That, slat, tap,
slap. You won, and then you lost. It is
about allocating. Results. Last word, very
briefly. Many thanks to. Ghosts of hydrangeas.
Are brittle networks of something fused.
Hidden under green, white bones. But lighter,
these nets flicker and tremble in funnels.
The air is sweet, moving. Quiet, if peeled off
from all those. Growls and rushes, sound of.
A sheet turning, singly. What is being read.
Slowly, without reason. Take it as time is.
A spray, it can sometimes well up. Endlessly
into detail, or break off. Without thought of
distribution, generous in itself. Smoothness
of peaches. Soapstone. Bite, suck in the juice.
Thickness of showers, each drop caught by
thirsty tongues. Scrabbling up the pines, or
the flick of hot tails on bare slabs. Did they
only stay, without thought of. What moved.
Among the rocks, riding out of cities.
Noticing the book as long as his arm. An
interruption of living continuously spoken.
Is always heretical, whichever way you look.

8 AUGUST

74

VII

White wings bleed at the edge. Species
thought drowned. In fierce night illumination,
comes out yellow. Clusters under the tap,
unyielding. Stones, propelled out in the day.
Would they prefer. Freedom, differently
managed. Today, under heavier skies. Quag
chute filled with thick waters. Not yet out
with the tide, or yet. To reduce gradually.
Spent. Listening to seabirds not heard on the
hill. Not one obliging, this estuarine fantasy
does figure as egress. Blocked, knowing the
rise and fall. Does mean movement elsewhere,
riverine trust. Is instrumental, a gauge of
settling and removal. Where veins answer in
flows and races, then ebb. Do you wait for
return. Beyond the bleariness of sleep, day.
Rolls unconsciously, without depths of. Any
measure to concern you. Beyond thick waters,
creekside stupors, construction is. Relentless
crane talk, piling down. Girders are ribs, split
open, a loom. For grey light, distant untenancy.
Where lungs might be. Expected, no interior
air occupancy lifting. Future expressions of
living. Beyond the concrete, humming. Small
voices, they may hide. Stashing themselves
in pockets of other stories, dubbing out. Do
you see the work of lips and tongues. Moments
of hesitation look fake, there to convince.

14 AUGUST

VIII

Cut back. Briars grow quickly, snake. Across
the path. Grass is matted in hanks, rain is due.
It falls. Oak apples, city grit. Are we done with
summer, they say. It arrived briefly, seen off.
In clouds of harlequins, not staying. Long enough
to breed, doors stick in the damp. Black moons
behind the nails, stains of. Sweet black fruit,
heavy. Where the small oak weighs down in dust.
He picks them gingerly, pound for pound. It is not
how it was, warmer then and a low red sun. Lost.
Behind the hollow grass, straw dry. The edge of.
Autumn was coming on, cool mist on skin. Decay
is a natural shame, it embarrasses. What you thought
to. Hold together, confidence in. Seasons, running
ahead. While. There are banks of growing to do.
Some still in flower, others are green fruit, this is.
A composite pain, it is what is. Skipped out unknowing
in the avoidance of bees, the approach of gargoyles.
He says, I saw this stone before, it haunts me
in the grass. Relishing the chill, did you. See it there
too. Today, what creeps while. You don't look. So
many in the dust, not recovered. As retribution for.
Retribution, for. Is it her among the stalks, did she.
Bend down to take what had been missed, or reach.
For dark berries hanging over thorns, did she. Crush
them in her fingers. As ripeness singles them out for
taking, not knowing the feint of. Harvest, its matter.
Drawing in a child's hand those red round suns.

15 AUGUST

Dark roaming. Panthers, are they inside or out. Stalking
moors, disguised. Night beasts, the shadow of a long line.
Lengthens. The way a tail crooks, shoulders mass. Intent,
otherwise. Suburban, breaks through privets to pick off
unsuspecting. Wanderers, sent scattering. With delightful
screams. Upended cones, mint chocolate chip. Ice. Melting
over hanging steps, where. Sea leaches out from under.
Concrete, at high tide, salt ambivalences. Does it return
already. Or give way to vertical rockpools, waves of purple.
Undulating. Did you set them loose. Are they inside, gleaming.
Amber, fur insistencies. Forcing the frame, hold it. Back,
where retreat leaves lives exposed. Piles of bladderwrack
not dry enough to pop, she squeezes pockets of air. Pursing
each one, why. Not bubblewrap, why. Does this shell inch
rapidly. Hermit disappointment. I could lay on the board,
float out. Beyond where it took me. Past usual summer limits,
cove anxieties. Mew stones. Flocks of calling birds, turning
away from. Shore noises. Damming the stream, lugging
boulders, big enough to. Bruise small limbs, she has longed
to. Run in to the water with the others. Cries silently.
Wrapped. Step over to where the wet sand sheens, pick
out. Every stone marked by a circle. Step in to. Temporary
holding patterns, the rill of them. Under bare feet, hers
lifted limp. Heron on the bank had long pins bent. Chip of
smooth turquoise glints for several seconds. Mottled,
the scrawl of birds' eggs. Flecks of. Caught in rock or
later, limestone pavements, cut through transverse. Door,
a peacock's tail. Carved. Padding, silently outside.

24 AUGUST

Still it comes preening, broad leaved. Absorbance
in stories of green filled. Flash floods. Risk this
rapid recombination, rain coursing down a bus
window. 1967. Reach for the bell, long line of cord.
Weeping under dryers, women's faces. Caught with.
All that hair cropped. You look so old. Doesn't she.
Dust falls in the middle of oceans, thousands of miles
from. Where it began. Injuring astronomical instruments
and eyes, full of. Infusoria. No less than sixty-seven.
Different organic forms. Inhabiting the obscurity of.
Pile them up, reported. Remembrances, pebbles stack.
If removed are subject to litigation. Pile them up on the
sill. Swallows are leaving early, they say. In search of.
Summer, dry carcasses woven. Wasp, moth, harlequin,
web hibernation is premature, tell them earnestly. In cases
of aerial transparency. Depth is blue, how far we look.
Taking cuttings from the common. In to the welkin, it
is a glowing drum. Then darkness comes in a low hiss.
Distant voices carry hesitations, are forceful. Raised
to silence. Black burr of heat stills. Engine on the hill
shifts gears during encounters in August. Frequencies of
insects, larger than customary. Dragonfly with black
net wings. Spent time on the damp washing, it batted
against. My hand, hung for many minutes. Try to
capture it, the battery is failing. He exclaimed, see
how large it is. Throbbing. Yellow streak abdomen.
It will not come again. Hatched in distant waters. Now,
morning. Wind lifts a million husks. Shhhhhhh.

26 August

Grasshopper, sitting on his palm. A straw quill.
Masters calm, triumph. In time, finally. Overcome,
what jumps. From moment to. Is stilled, does he
feel. The gift of it, too soon. Not yet. Understood,
the second sits. Paler than the first. Colour of hills
and grasses, track through to. Familiar avenues but
this is discovery in minutest. Extension, our road
is a line beyond. The wall, it requires a letting down.
From fields and spaces, the possibility of a world.
Without torture, or. Impulsion suddenly. Sitting on
the steadiness of flesh equations, because we. Might
find it consonant, and not divided further. Up there
on the bank, where the track. Winds unknowing.
Scrub and gravel, the hum of. Seeing us cross with
a box of berries. Reluctant, but in repetition, seeds
catch. In the teeth, the sun snags sometimes. Too,
collecting nothing, stained, that is the point. His full
heart needs, today. Did you find out who cracked
the pot, asking. Was it the roots. Five pieces neatly
arranged, I replaced the hydrangea this morning.
She said, so solicitous. Thorns do piece your skirt,
fiercer sometimes than you can manage. To unhook,
expanding. Surface undergrowth, in preparation for
a flaying of. Minutes taken. Voices are louder where
they encounter. Bodilessly. Without shame of. Fallen
apples suggest. A lost inhabiting, a plastic tent was
rigged seasons back. In deeper bushes, do you live off
this land, too lightly. Outlived, fleet when prompted.

27 AUGUST

XII

Sounds, webbed air. Tell me there are ribs, beneath
this. Muscular beating. Sending it interrupted. Does
each word have its day, under the planes. The bolus of
a seed falls, large as an eye. Already moving off,
impulsively. To begin, where. Girth of light, hidden
in a cloud. Is splitting among all these congregations.
Did you see. How we all expanded consequently. Finding
each sound was a splinter, a small window. Where you
peer out. Or more than one, gathered. A cluster of, is it.
Warm, flesh looking. Spread equal to the turn of the.
Afternoon, its slow pivot. Wheeling with. Accommodations,
gently. Lifted, susurrus. High branching of. Skirts and canopies,
planetary yawl, you would know that. This is a giant ball,
flung and spinning. And we sit, words accumulating,
drift. Down the hedgerows, seeded as cotton is, lightly.
Thinking someone had strewn them, cleaning off makeup.
But they were real, and floating. Nature, spilling over,
the necessity of waste as a kind of freedom. Or play, that
might not have an end. At this hour, they fly up hopefully.
Or peck underfoot. Untroubled by. Guns and accidents,
going on. Affirming, where pain is. Our constant, branded
in. Skin and bark. Arrest, surprise at how lightness comes upon.
Everyone, when so much. Falls. Heavily, or brushes against.
Flocking, the rush overhead. Is always a flight inside, keeping
its quiet. Trajectory insistent, that it might take off. For distant
branches, set organs. In a chorus, the way they aim at head
height, disconcerts. Do you flinch at the astonishment of
beating wings, air explosions. Waves of fallout, laughter.

30 AUGUST

XIII

Time spent. Drawing mountains is unrewarding.
Already too vertiginous. To manage, the high route.
Disturbs, cold crevasses, opening in. Thought, not
for the faint. Future journeys seem unlikely. To make
them more than triangular. On the page, nor spoken.
Call them flowers, as he would. Or pleat them where
divisions might not seem. Fatal to space, where you
live it. How did they do that, roped. Together, in
skirts. Prefer the long view, then comes. Now, when
you could get closer. In the foothills, obscure mist
in daily webcasts. Will that be possible vision, is it.
Managed, or a limit. Stepped into, where you hoped
for more clarity. It is a cool day. Stories of arrival.
Rope reeling machine cuts the honest boy in half.
Labour is a tap, it runs in glacial measures. Scraping
in its wake, then pouring uncontrollably in outwash.
There is no safe. Harbour. Crushes where flesh gives
way. To life, without safeguards. Leaving us all
hanging, somewhere in the depths. Axed, is that a
metaphor. For trees or ropes, cut away. From all
that holds up. Or together, bonds woven. That long
scream. Always in movies when they. Drop, in
deep focus. Span of something real suggested in.
Attenuated voices, the way they shrink down to a
thread. Is a measurement without echo. Despite
reverberations, a quick in sound. Is it why
the fates had scissors, according to. Mountain
oracles, rendering ends domestic in polis vertigo.

31 AUGUST

XIV

Sometimes see cities far off. Lip of clouds furling
over, as if waves have whipped up. Disastrously,
to make the heart beat faster. There is nothing you
could do, it is. A grand rendition of rescue, rolling
in. Aerial finality, you cannot. Take in the breath
it would need. To survive it, there. On Mount Tam,
the stones were green. The laurels were ancient,
vision marked the extent of memorials. Without
limits, over the clam beds, returning. To a city
without elevation, where. Sawing of cherry trees
brings down the large branches. In redaction, for
brown site dealings. That we all might shake down,
waiting for the deluge. To fuse us into saltflats, eels
purling at warm outflow, growing larger than. Is
demanded rightfully. Ladders shuddering, tides
of white trumpets. Taking over, rills of. Back wall
eddying, looking up at what passes for sky. Scale of
ants and magpies, mine. Today, squinting up at.
Sunlight, its intermittence. Where sight falters in
brick geometries, held up. While a slow stream
moves. Northwards, by giant steps. There it made
you weep to be part of. A flow without end, so
that you might. Already be climbing there, pillion.
Seeing it for the first time, that removal from. Cities.
And still, at once. At a point in a future, the young
woman. Seeing her wedding taking place, hearing
the crunch of tyres on gravel, taking crystal to the
clam beds. Today, without it striking in the heart.

1 SEPTEMBER

Brown coffee. Scent of warm breeze, season
turning gratefully. How much time passes finding
the route. To the park gates. Synchrony of boys,
passage of limbs. Send them out simultaneous,
seeds burst from the pod. In freefall, owning the
space they pass over. Bees do like urban hives, she
had to bring herself. To return when taken in. By
their doziness, batting up against skin. Stung at
harvest time, leaving pollen. Inoculations, clouding
slightly. To secure every comfort in environments.
Thought, leaves. Begin to shed, slight tinge in the lilac,
green still holds. Hinging the year, from the first seen.
They visit and are heavy. How to keep themselves
flying, when. Gleaning, legs fat and colliding with
masonry. Drunk with late summer. The bee crawls
slowly, it may end here. Deep in the grass, finding.
It has reached an unexpected point. Of determination,
which is the duration of an end, where it begins.
Another slow climb. The same but disassembled,
boy. Numbers the conkers, too early falling. Naming
each its number. Is *this* one. Is *this* two. And *this*.
Does the bee tally, what is it. Weighed with. Carrying
enumerations, on account. Of a pattern, accreting.
Singular. *This*. Dark bolt. Nothing in its path, finally.
But its own blind relation, it throbs. Where fear of
breathing might be interpreted. In premonition of.
Its abdomen arches, it throbs. The truth of organisms
is. This breathing goes on, until it does not, strongly.

3 SEPTEMBER

XVI

Cat waits, stretches. Shrinking densely by
the door. What it pinions by undetectable
scent, no-one knows how. Fear arrives, b-movie
id lurking brought on. Daily, it comes through
the perimeter fence, voiceless radiation, sits
washing itself. While sensory equipment judders.
Life signs. It will be mayhem. He said happily,
when she arrives. You do not walk with me any.
More, this morning is. Taking place, it sweats,
golden. Grey. Overcast, so very still. Everything
listens, knows movement goes on, elsewhere.
Instruments spike at the slightest breath. Or at
what is stricken, sonorous. Without balance. Is
silence a damming up of. Relief, cutting trees and
animals on paper. Or a catching in the throat,
pollen dust, detritus of what remains. In feeling.
It could have been. You are safely arrived, rescue
delivers. In overhanging bushes, cradled. Without
gratefulness, scarper. Before written warnings.
Which is to say, too late. For this season already
the air is turning, brief. Edge of smoke, cured in
nightfall. Clear skies, fronds of light. Usual skirl of
alarm makes the city a bowl. Morning is a crush
of clouds. Cold molten breaking. Flight of. Crows
suddenly noticed. Breaks through, the nap. Is
brushed against. Where the man wheeled his
mesh. Cloak, dancing, from beneath. I saw sky,
his fibres bound. Taut. Red against the open.

13 SEPTEMBER

XVII

Pale green light falls. Slow mounting in
reflected shadows, where palms grow only.
In some dark negative. Tropics, flushed full
with. Rain from the north, do you find them
pricked out. Under the skin, in veins. Are
world's weals. Tell me. Where something
blows, the pressure of breath is. Constant,
without lack of. Detail, or puncture, it rouses
you always. To attention in proposing. Surface
blitheness, lathes of sun. Begin again, crash
on the hill. Roiling, planes. Swing, bees in a
sound box. Drop from the line, it is a lost
sequence. Yodelling to intermittent hammers.
Tell me you come looking. Today, freely. Can
I stay until. Sports shoot from the base, smooth
of thorns. Wind beyond limits of what belongs.
Carefully paved and broken. Do you step on
the cracks to indrawn. Consternation, he said.
Until four. The way dancing spreads your
shoulders, is never enough. And forgotten, they
all remembered. When the reach came, it felt
as love does. Did they know, even when turning.
Away, to the smallness of objects. Ivy spreads in
swarms and tendrils, choking generously. Sit with
me and I can. Listen, still ringing from the night.
Arrives, property in the dark. Among roosting
birds. Steam rises from the cup. Tell me who is.
Here, now. *This*. When my sheet is full.

14 SEPTEMBER 2007

Selected REALITY STREET titles in print

Poetry series

Maggie O'Sullivan (ed.): *Out of Everywhere* (1996)
Denise Riley: *Selected Poems* (2000)
Ken Edwards: *eight + six* (2003)
David Miller: *Spiritual Letters (I-II)* (2004)
Redell Olsen: *Secure Portable Space* (2004)
Peter Riley: *Excavations* (2004)
Allen Fisher: *Place* (2005)
Tony Baker: *In Transit* (2005)
Jeff Hilson: *stretchers* (2006)
Maurice Scully: *Sonata* (2006)
Maggie O'Sullivan: *Body of Work* (2006)
Sarah Riggs: *chain of minuscule decisions in the form of a feeling* (2007)
Carol Watts: *Wrack* (2007)
Jeff Hilson (ed.): *The Reality Street Book of Sonnets* (2008)
Peter Jaeger: *Rapid Eye Movement* (2009)
Wendy Mulford: *The Land Between* (2009)
Allan K Horwitz/Ken Edwards (ed.): *Botsotso* (2009)
Bill Griffiths: *Collected Earlier Poems* (2010)
Fanny Howe: *Emergence* (2010)
Jim Goar: *Seoul Bus Poems* (2010)
James Davies: *Plants* (2011)

Narrative series

Ken Edwards: *Futures* (1998, reprinted 2010)
John Hall: *Apricot Pages* (2005)
David Miller: *The Dorothy and Benno Stories* (2005)
Douglas Oliver: *Whisper 'Louise'* (2005)
Ken Edwards: *Nostalgia for Unknown Cities* (2007)
Paul Griffiths: *let me tell you* (2008)
John Gilmore: *Head of a Man* (2011)

Go to www.realitystreet.co.uk, email info@realitystreet.co.uk or write to the address on the reverse of the title page for updates.

REALITY STREET depends for its continuing existence on the Reality Street Supporters scheme. For details of how to become a Reality Street Supporter, or to be put on the mailing list for news of forthcoming publications, write to the address on the reverse of the title page, or email **info@realitystreet.co.uk**

Visit our website at: **www.realitystreet.co.uk**

Reality Street Supporters who have sponsored this book:

David Annwn
Andrew Brewerton
Peter Brown
Clive Bush
John Cayley
Adrian Clarke
Dane Cobain
Tony Cullen
Ian Davidson
David Dowker
Derek Eales
Michael Finnissy
Allen Fisher
Sarah Gall
John Gilmore
John Goodby
Giles Goodland
Paul Griffiths
Charles Hadfield
Catherine Hales
John Hall
Alan Halsey
Robert Hampson
Randolph Healy
Simon Howard
Fanny Howe
Peter Hughes
Romana Huk

Elizabeth James & Harry Gilonis
L Kiew
Peter Larkin
Sang-yeon Lee/Jim Goar
Richard Leigh
Alan Loney
Tony Lopez
Chris Lord
Ian McMillan
Michael Mann
Peter Manson
Deborah Meadows
Geraldine Monk
Sean Pemberton
Pete & Lyn
Tom Quale
Josh Robinson
Lou Rowan
Will Rowe
Robert Sheppard
Peterjon & Yasmin Skelt
Hazel Smith
Harriet Tarlo
Alan Teder
Sam Ward
Susan Wheeler
John Wilkinson
Anonymous: 10

Lightning Source UK Ltd.
Milton Keynes UK
UKOW02f2251101116

287383UK00001B/122/P